HYDROPONICS

FOR ABSOLUTE BEGINNERS:

How Build Your Inexpensive Garden

Without Soil Fast and Easy

James Water

© Copyright 2020 - All rights reserved.

The content contained within this book may not be reproduced, duplicated, or transmitted without direct written permission from the author or the publisher.Under no circumstances will any blame or legal responsibility be held against the publisher, or author, for any damages, reparation, or monetary loss due to the information contained within this book. Either directly or indirectly. Legal Notice:This book is copyright protected. This book is only for personal use. You cannot amend, distribute, sell, use, quote or paraphrase any part, or the content within this book, without the consent of the author or publisher. Disclaimer Notice:Please note the information contained within this document is for educational and entertainment purposes only. All effort has been executed to present accurate, up to date, and reliable, complete information. No warranties of any kind are declared or implied. Readers acknowledge that the author is not engaging in the rendering of legal, financial, medical, or professional advice. The content within this book has been derived from various sources. Please consult a licensed professional before attempting any techniques outlined in this book.By reading this document, the reader agrees that under no circumstances is the author responsible for any losses, direct or indirect, which are incurred as a result of the use of the information contained within this document, including, but not limited to, — errors, omissions, or inaccuracies.

Table of Content

Chapter 1 — 5
HYDROPONIC CULTIVATION — 5

Chapter 2 — 9
HISTORY — 9

Chapter 3 — 19
THE ADVANTAGES AND DISADVANTAGES OF HYDROPONIC CULTURES — 19

Chapter 4 — 23
TECHNIQUES FOR HYDROPONIC CULTIVATION — 23

4.1 Hydroponic cultivation technique in DWC — 24

4.2 Hydroponic cultivation technique NFT — 27

4.3 Hydroponic cultivation technique in Dutch Bucket — 29

4.4 Hydroponic cultivation technique on coconut coir — 31

4.5 Kratky method — 33

4.6 Wick system — 38

4.7 Ebb and Flow — 44

4.8 Drip system — 49

4.9 Vertical system — 52

4.10 Fogponics — 56

4.11 Conclusions — 62

Chapter 5 — 63
STARTING CULTIVATION WITH HYDROPONIC TECHNIQUE — 63

5.1 Necessary to Start Hydroponic Cultivation — 63

5.2 Preparation of the germination area — 68

5.3 Installation of the Hydroponic System and Sprout Housing — 71

5.4 The lighting system _____ 75

5.5 Set up the Grow Room_____ 84

5.6 The Light in the Grow Room _____ 86

5.7 Temperature in the Grow Room _____ 90

5.8 Grow Room moisture_____ 93

5.9 The Ventilation of the Grow Room _____ 95

5.10 Water Quality in Hydroponic: PH, EC, and Temperature_____ 98

5.11 Fertilization of Hydroponics_____ 103

Chapter 6 _____ 107

BEST PLANTS FOR HYDROPONICS _____ 107

6.1 Lettuce _____ 110

6.2 Strawberries_____ 116

6.3 Tomatoes _____ 120

6.4 Kitchen herbs _____ 122

6.5 Orchids _____ 125

6.6 Plants to avoid in Hydroponic cultivation _____ 128

Chapter 7 _____ 131

HYDROPONICS VS AQUAPONICS _____ 131

Chapter 8 _____ 139

HYDROPONICS VS AEROPONICS _____ 139

Chapter 9 _____ 145

IT'S TIME TO TRY!_____ 145

Chapter 1

HYDROPONIC CULTIVATION

Hydroponics is a generic term that embraces different cultivation techniques that have as a standard feature the use of water and nutrients to feed plants that are grown "out of the soil" or without using the land.

There are two main methods of hydroponic cultivation; the first foresees the use of "inert" materials or supports whose purpose is only to support the root system of the plant, the other is the direct immersion of the roots in the nutrient solution.

The advantages of hydroponic without soil cultivation - compared to traditional cultivation techniques - lie above all in the possibility of starting one or more hydroponic crops even in less hospitable environments and in conditions not suitable for the birth and growth of plants. For example, it is indicated in all those places characterized by a high drought or where temperatures are particularly rigid or in areas where the soil under excessively sandy, rocky, or arid.

Amount of water to be provided for irrigation

Another essential aspect of hydroponic cultivation fundamental for fans and professionals of hydroponic gardening is the quantity of water to be provided for irrigation: in traditional crops on the land, the amount of water necessary to be able to cultivate and make the plants fruit is clearly higher compared to that required by vegetables grown in hydroponics. In fact, it is calculated that the ratio is 10 (for traditional crops) to 1 (for hydroponic crops).

Hydroponic culture

The saving of water is reflected both in the economic aspect and on the environmental issue.

In short, hydroponic cultivation - also known as hydroponic culture precisely because it affects different economic, social, and even cultural areas - has a decidedly limited ecological footprint compared to traditional cultivation techniques.

Use of fertilizers, herbicides, and pesticides

Another critical factor is the use of fertilizers, herbicides, and pesticides used and the relative quantities foreseen in the two types of crops: the volumes of fertilizers used are somewhat limited and always well targeted. Furthermore, there is no dispersion of the soil. Herbicides are not used, because they are not necessary, while pesticides are used in small quantities.

Organic Hydroponic cultivation

For those who want to grow organically, it is possible to use organic fertilizers that allow you to have a hydroponic organic culture, respecting health, and the environment.

Why choose a Hydroponic cultivation method?

In a hydroponic system, plants grow out of the ground, in a fully regulated crop context and free from pests and diseases from the soil.

By controlling environmental parameters, such as light, nutrients, temperature, pH, and conductivity, results are obtained much higher than traditional crops, without having to use pesticides that often produce harmful effects on the culture itself.

The hydroponic cultivation technique maximizes the yield in terms of quality, quantity, and speed. For this reason, hydroponic crops are becoming increasingly popular and appreciated not only by professionals and large distribution chains (we point out that most of the tomatoes on sale today in supermarkets come from hydroponics) both from small direct growers and - for pleasure or work - they decide to try their hand at crops of this type.

Chapter 2

HISTORY

"INVENTED BY THE BABYLONIANS AND THE AZTECS"

The hydroponic cultivation technique has deep roots in the history of humanity and arises from particular needs. In the 21st century, with the increase in specific needs, it is still topical. Indeed, interest is renewed today.

The first examples of soilless cultivation can be considered the hanging gardens of the Babylonians or the floating ones of the Aztecs of Mexico and the Chinese.

The Aztecs did not have arable land; for this, they implemented an ingenious system to use the existing lake in their territory. They built rafts of reeds and rushes tied together. On them, they placed fertile soil dredged from the bottom of the lake and used it to grow different vegetables. These rafts were often connected and sometimes brought the gardener's home. The plants emitted the roots that headed towards the lake water. At the time of sale of the products, the raft was brought to the marketplace. This cultivation system was used until the 19th century.

More scientific forms of hydroculture began in the 17th century. The Englishman John Woodward (1699) is usually referred to as the first person to have raised plants in a nutrient solution.

Starting in the early 19th century, scholars began to understand that plants need nitrogen, potassium, phosphorus, calcium, sulfur, and iron. Later, around 1860, two German plant physiologists, Sachs and Knop, recognizing how difficult it was to qualitatively and quantitatively study the essential elements in plants grown in a medium as complex as the soil, cultivated plants with their roots immersed in a solution of salts. Minerals (a nutrient solution), whose chemical composition was controlled within limits set by the purity of the chemicals then available. Other researchers later showed that growth improved if the roots were aerated. However, these were practices restricted to laboratories and aimed at studying plant growth and nutrition.

In 1929, William Frederick Gericke, a plant physiologist from the University of California (Berkeley), proposed using water culture methods to produce cultivated plants on a commercial scale, rather than as a research tool. He called the technique "aquaculture." Gericke later in 1937, at the suggestion of Setchell of the University of California, announced that the method was to be called "hydroponics" since the term water-culture had previously been defined as the breeding of plants and aquatic animals.

Setchell called hydroponics "the art and science of crop production in a liquid culture medium." Hydroponics derives from the Greek hydro, which means water and ponos, which means work (literally water that works) and is analogous to the word "geoponics," the ancient term for agriculture. Other and new terms were coined later, such as "nutriculture" and "chemiculture," all indicating the principle illustrated above. In hydroponics, Gericke cultivated vegetables (chard, radish, carrot, potato, etc.), cereals, ornamental and fruit plants, as well as flowers. Using large tanks, he successfully bred tomato plants over 7m long in his laboratory.

In 1936 Gericke and Tavernetti showed that by heating the nutrient solution, it was possible to grow the tomato throughout the year and produce fruit for 8-9 months. They also stated that the potential yields of tomato grown in nutrient solutions were many times larger than those obtained on soil due to the higher density and height of the plants as well as the longer duration of the growing period

In the late 1930s, two of the leading scientists of the University of California, Hoagland, and Arnon, were commissioned to study hydroponics and, in 1938, published the bulletin on "nutriculture," a term that included all the methods for growing plants in a medium other than natural soil.

One of the first successes of hydroponics was in 1930 on the island of Wake, a rocky atoll in the Pacific, stopping point for transoceanic flights. On that island, the production of hydroponic vegetables was the only practical method of obtaining fresh vegetables for the passengers and crew of Pan America Airways. Fresh vegetables could not be shipped to the island of Wake, due to the high costs, and could not be bred because of the lack of land. Hydroponics represented an ideal solution.

Subsequently, this technology was used in some limited applications on the Atlantic and Pacific islands during the Second World War.

After the war, the University of Purdue spread hydroponics (called nutricolture) in a series of popular bulletins that described in detail the nutrient solutions for both liquid and aggregate systems (in solid medium).

Despite the commercial interest, these cultivation systems did not spread due to the high costs for the construction of the cultivation benches.

After about 20 years, interest in hydroponics was renewed thanks to the advent of plastics that were used not only in greenhouse covers but also in cultivation products. And they were also crucial for the introduction of drip irrigation.

Sericulture began to expand significantly in Europe and Asia during the 1950s and 1960s, and relevant hydroponic systems were experienced in California, Arizona, Abu Dhabi, and Iran in the 1970s. In these desert locations, the benefits of technology were motivated by the durability and advantage of solar radiation, which maximized photosynthetic production. Unfortunately, the oil crisis that began in 1973 increased the costs for heating and cooling controlled environment agriculture by 1-2 orders of magnitude. This, together with the few chemicals registered for the control of pathogens, caused more than one failure and diminished the interest in hydroponics, especially in the USA.

However, research on hydroponics has continued. In the late 1970s, researchers from the Glasshouse Crops Research Institute in Great Britain developed the nutrient film technique (NFT).

After 20 years, interest in soilless crops seems renewed both among researchers and among farmers, especially in areas where there is more significant concern about the pollution of groundwater caused by fertilizers and the use of chemicals for soil disinfection.

Today, although hydroponics is still a system little used with respect to the quantity of soil dedicated to protected crops, it is thought that, in the short term, it will find more space in the agricultural panorama since some problems will be solved such as:

- the need to reduce production costs;

- the need to improve production;

- the increase in environmental pollution linked to intensive agriculture and the legislative constraints deriving from it;

- the lack of resources such as water, work, energy.

Chapter 3

THE ADVANTAGES AND DISADVANTAGES OF HYDROPONIC CULTURES

Soilless cultivation is a useful tool for controlling crop growth and production through mineral nutrition management.

The main advantages to be registered are:

1. Shortening of development times.

Hydroponic crops should be used in artificially illuminated environments or greenhouses to keep environmental conditions under control.

Precisely the respect of the necessary ecological conditions allows us to speed up the growth of the plants and to achieve maturation in less time. However, the possibility of using these systems in outdoor cultivation is not excluded.

Plants in a hydroponic system develop faster than a traditional method in the ground as there are more considerable attention and greater control of nutrients as well as a more prosperous supply of oxygen to the root system. By breathing more easily, plants accelerate their metabolism and take less time to grow.

The shortening of development times leads to a reduction in the number of hours of light and, therefore, the switching on of the lamps and the operation of the extractors, with a consequent decrease in the expenditure of electricity and an extension of the life of the system. Furthermore, the shorter the cycle, the less likely it is that diseases will develop;

2. Better working conditions from plant to harvest, also with control of the actual crop needs;

3. Productivity per meter higher, thanks to a higher density of seedlings and the elimination of the attack by soil pathogens.

4. Increase in post-harvest product quality.

The vegetables produced in hydroponics do not contain the remains of chemicals used for geosterilization, they are cleaner, and from a nutritional point of view, they do not show any difference with the products cultivated on the soil.

Hydroponics is considered an eco-compatible cultivation technique as it does not involve geosterilization, and inclosed cycles, the use of water and fertilizers is reduced.

The quality of agricultural and horticultural products has also made remarkable progress: the market appreciates not only the traditional aspects (freshness, taste, and flavor) but also aspects such as production conditions (environmental and social responsibility) and product safety.

Although hydroponic crops offer a number of undoubted advantages, they are not free from some disadvantages. The price of a system for hydroponic cultivation is higher than a traditional one.

The environment used in addition to having a higher cost also implies a higher maintenance expense. In addition to this disadvantage, the cost of electricity used for light, and the circulation of water significantly affects the final gain.

Although the process is straightforward, a good knowledge of the plants that you want to grow and the nutrients that will be used throughout the process is required. Without an adequate understanding of the substances to be used, all the plants in cultivation will lead to death in a short time.

After careful consideration of the various pros and cons that hydroponic cultivation systems offer, you will be able to determine if this type of cultivation is right for you.

Obviously, if the pros outweigh the cons, then you can choose to use this process. On the other hand, if you see it as a risky choice, then perhaps it is better to choose a more conventional method for your crops.

In the end, hydroponics has always been considered an efficient solution for the production of vegetables and plants.

Chapter 4

TECHNIQUES FOR HYDROPONIC CULTIVATION

When planning hydroponic cultivation, various factors must be taken into consideration, such as the type of plant (e.g., tomatoes, strawberries, or salad), the place where it will be mounted (indoor cultivation or external greenhouse), the size of the system or the environment.

The above factors influence the choice of the type of technique to be used. Here are some of them, none is the best, but each one is perfect to use according to a specific situation.

4.1 Hydroponic cultivation technique in DWC

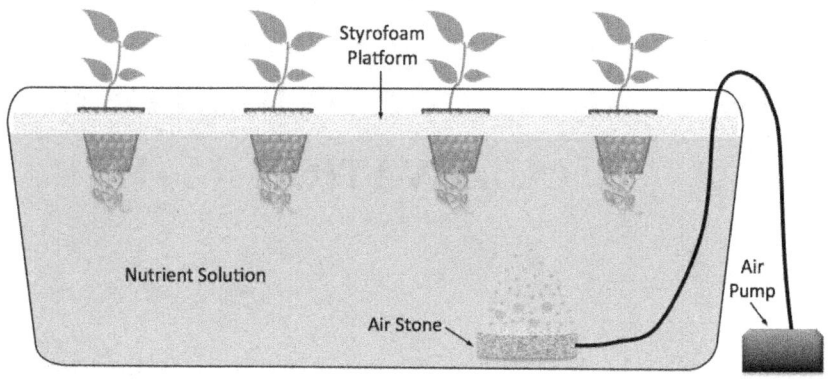

DWC, an acronym for Deep Water Culture, or deep water cultivation, is a hydroponic cultivation technique that consists of growing plants in a highly oxygenated solution based on water and fertilizers.

Compared to the other hydroponic cultivation methods, which use an inert substrate such as expanded clay, rock wool, perlite, etc. for radical propagation, in DWC the roots are completely (or almost) immersed within the solution that will do both substrates that act as a carrier for nutrients.

It is, therefore, possible to grow large plants with minimum use of the substrate, a fistful of expanded clay in which to make the young seedling take root and hold it till the roots coming out of the jar will be able to grow in the solution. For this reason, cultivation in deep water can be considered a middle ground between traditional hydroponics and aeroponics.

The advantages of growing in DWC can be summarized in:

-Accelerated growth, as the higher concentration of oxygen at the roots, stimulates the absorption of nutrients and the metabolism of the plant

-Increased production: plants grown in DWC have higher yields than those grown on land

-Minimum use of substratum: it will no longer be necessary to move large volumes of soil or other substrates as a.small amount of expanded clay is sufficient to grow large plants

-Little maintenance: there are no drips that could get clogged or water pumps that, in the event of a malfunction, would block the irrigation of the plants. Even in the event of a blackout, plants grown in DWC would survive.

Cultivation in deep water is best suited in those situations where the temperature can be controlled, in particular, that of the water; for this reason, they are well suited to be used indoors for the cultivation of medium or large plants. Instead, they are less suitable in very hot places, unless a solution refrigeration system such as a chiller is used.

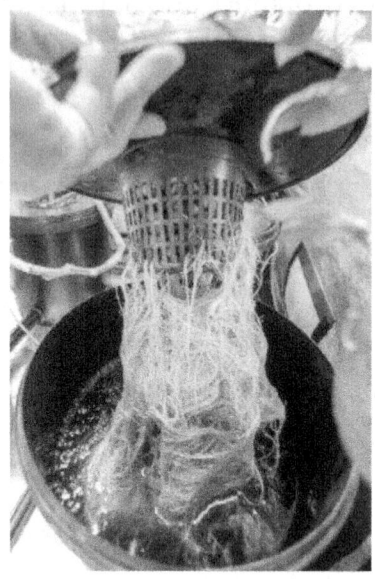

A variant of the cultivation in deep water is the so-called floating systems, mainly used for the cultivation of salads. The plants are on boards that float inside a tank, and the roots grow immersed in the solution and are oxygenated by movement pumps or aerators.

4.2 Hydroponic cultivation technique NFT

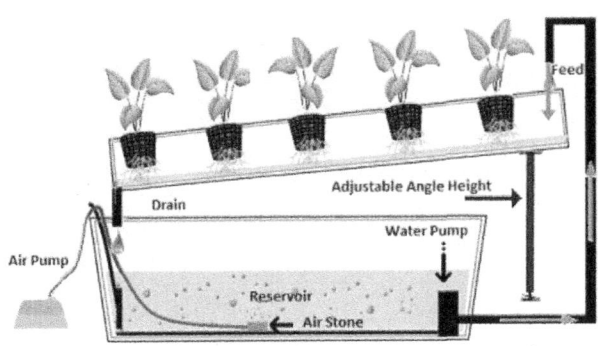

NFT, an acronym for Nutrient Film Technique, is based on the principle that the roots of the plant grow in contact with water that flows non-stop. In this way the roots themselves are non-stop enriched by the gaseous exchange with the oxygen present in the air and absorb the nutrients and oxygen present in the solution.

In general, these systems are made up of perforated conduits connected to a storage tank and a pump that continually keeps the solution circulating. It is crucial that the pump always works. In the event of a stop, the solution would cease to reach the roots, which could dry out in a few hours.

This system works very well with different types of plants, from salads to strawberries or larger plants, it is possible to adapt the size of the raceways and the distance of the holes, as well as the arrangement in the space in particular when you want to use it vertically.

4.3 Hydroponic cultivation technique in Dutch Bucket

It is a plastic bucket with a square or rectangular base, with a particular shape that allows it to be placed along a discharge line that leads to a storage tank. From this, the solution is distributed from above to each bucket through a pump. It irrigates the roots, and flows back through the drain channel.

In Dutch buckets, the roots of plants grow inside clay or perlite, materials with good draining power that allow a lot of air and, therefore, oxygen to pass through them.

Through drip trays, the plants receive the necessary water and nutrients. A siphon present at the bottom of each bucket ensures that a few centimeters of the solution are always available, which, in the event of a blackout, would be a reserve, giving the grower more time to intervene.

Another significant advantage is that they lend themselves to being assembled in a personalized way. It is possible to vary the distance between them, they can be arranged on different floors or to be easily moved from one place to another.

This system is reasonably easy to implement and lends itself very well to use in both home and commercial greenhouses.

4.4 Hydroponic cultivation technique on coconut coir

Coconut is a substrate with excellent characteristics for hydroponic cultivation. It has good water retention, protects the root system and at the same time offers a remarkable passage of air and therefore better oxygenation

The coconut fiber before being used for this purpose is washed and filtered, then dehydrated and compacted into blocks or slabs that make it convenient for storage.

Before being reused, these must be rehydrated; at this point, the fiber will absorb the water, increasing in volume up to 5 times.

Being an inert substrate, therefore devoid of nutrients, these must be supplied through a nutrient solution, which will be administered at intervals through drippers with a series of daily cycles.

Another significant advantage is the possibility of being reused and being able to grow for 2 or 3 cycles with the same substrate.

The coconut plates are suitable for the cultivation of all plants, and in particular, they are trendy in the cultivation of strawberries. The slabs can be arranged on raceways or overhead supports that make the cultivator's job more comfortable as well as harvesting.

4.5 Kratky method

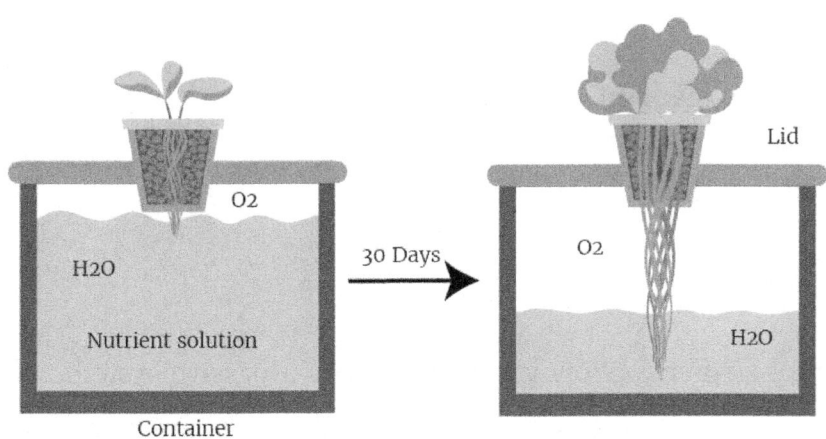

The first system we recommend for creating a hydroponic garden is the famous Kratky method. It is undoubtedly one of the simplest, suitable for those approaching Hydroponics for the first time and is ideal for those who want to grow vegetables.

With this system, you can grow vegetables such as lettuce and spinach. It is also a system suitable for growing tomatoes.

For its realization, the following materials are needed:

- a mason jar, container, or bucket;

- seed starter cubes;

- growing medium (Hydroton works well);

- Net Pots;

- PH kit.

These elements allow you to configure a passive system, which does not require electricity and which can operate for several weeks without maintenance.

That's it, other than water and nutrients.

First, you should have a seedling ready. The seedling can be cultivated in a seed starter cube. The roots should start to become visible on the bottom of the cube before transplanting.

You can only use one plant per seed starting cube and one per net pot.

You can grow all kinds of plants using the Kratky method, from tomatoes to lettuce. You need a three to five-gallon bucket for tomatoes or cucumbers and a mason jar or a plastic soda bottle for lettuce. I advise using wide mouth mason jars with 3-inch net pots.

The Kratky method is a set and forget growing method you can use on your windowsill. Once the plant starts to grow, the level in the container will drop. As the roots grow, they will keep up with the lowering water level. This will continue until the plant is fully grown. Lettuce needs around sixteen fluid ounces (four hundred and seventy-five milliliters), while the three to five-gallon (eleven to eighteen liter) bucket for tomatoes needs to be refilled often.

The roots will take up the water, and the plant will start to grow. The nutrient solution will drain, but the roots will keep up with the draining water level.

The empty space that is created will provide the roots with oxygen. This will continue until the plant is fully matured, and the water has drained. You need to aim for the plant growth to keep up with the water in the reservoir.

You need to place the setup in a well-lit environment. You must darken the outside of the container with tin foil. This is to discourage algae from growing in the container. Do not use black paper or paint because it will heat the water in the box.

If the water has entirely drained while your plant is not fully grown yet, you need to top-up the water. You need to fill it up halfway, so only half of the roots are submerged.

This system can be established virtually anywhere and needs very little space. I recommend trying this setup for everyone who is starting with Hydroponics.

Build the system

Smaller plants:

Take a two or three-inch net pot and put some Hydroton at the bottom. Place your seedling with the seed starter cube in the net pot. Fill the sides with Hydroton for the cube to stay upright. Fill the nutrient solution in the container until it touches the bottom of the seed starting cube. Darken the water container so no algae will grow inside.

Bigger plants:

Use a three or five-gallon bucket and use a six-inch net pot with a lid. The process is the same as the smaller plant. The six-inch net pot will be more natural for the plant to hold onto because the root system will be much more significant.

If you refill the bucket, only fill it up halfway. This is for the roots to access oxygen. If you were to submerge the whole root system, root rot would occur, and your plant will die.

4.6 Wick system

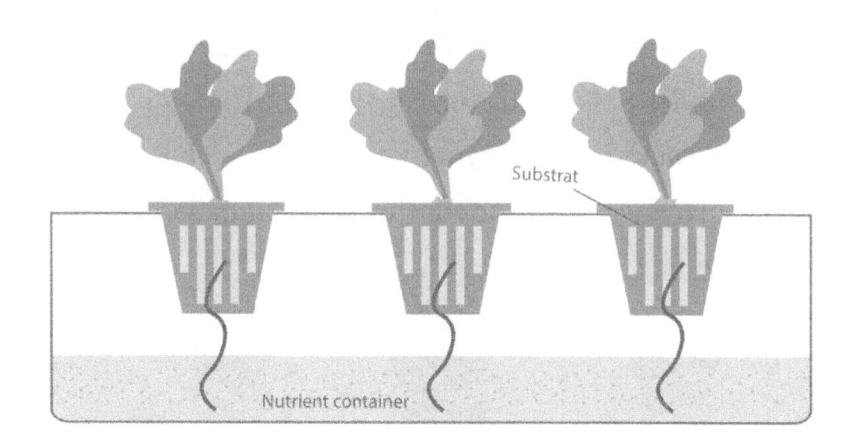

Substrat

Nutrient container

Simple, passive Hydroponic system.

The wick system is another easy system to make hydroponic growth.

It doesn't have any moving parts, and there is no reliance on electricity.

The plant is cultured in a substratum, which is supplied with a nutrient solution by the capillary action of the wick.

This is a straightforward system to build and one that will give you a great introduction to Hydroponics. It's very similar to the Kratky method but with the addition of a wick.

You will need:

- a plastic bottle or tub with lid;

- two-inch net pots;

- seed starter cube;

- growing media of your choice;

- wicking rope.

Building the Wick system

The water container has the water and nutrients a plant needs. Above this sits the plant and a wicking rope that will bring water and nutrients to the plant using the capillary action of the wick.

Start by drilling two-inch holes in the top of your lid. Drill as many as you need to fill the top of the lid. Don't forget that your seedlings will grow, so take that into account. Lettuce, for example, should be six to eight inches apart from each other (center to center) depending on the variety.

Start by filling your container with water and nutrient solution.

Take the two-inch net pots and put the wicking rope trough, so it touches the grow media. Make sure it will touch the roots of the seedling you are going to put in.

Place the lid on the container and place the net cups into the holes you drilled. The wick will be inside the water solution. If done correctly, the wick will deliver the nutrient-rich water to the plant roots. Make this wick touch the bottom of the water reservoir. As the water slowly drains, the wick will provide water to the roots.

This is a good system for slightly smaller plants, such as lettuce and herbs. However, it is not very practical for more substantial plants like tomatoes, fruiting plants, and peppers. These tend to need an abundant supply of water and nutrients. The wick system may not be able to deliver them fast enough.

If you choose to create a wick system, you need to consider the right wick material carefully. It is worth testing a few and always soak them first to ensure they provide the most effective wicking action possible.

The best option found is using a thick candlewick. They are designed to wick up wax and are made of cotton. They are quite thick too. A roll of six feet will cost you $6. You can reuse these also.

You can make the reservoir as large as you like and increase the number of plants you have accordingly.

It is also important to underline that the wick will absorb water and nutrients evenly, but your plant may not. If the air is warmer than usual, the plant will evaporate more water than when it's colder. The evaporation will lead to water being drawn from the wick without the nutrients.

This can result in a build-up of nutrients on the wick, which will damage the ability of the wick to work effectively. Therefore, you should wash or rinse your wick after every harvest to remove excess nutrients (nutrient build-up).

Make sure you block the sun or your grow light from entering the water container. Wrap something around it for the light not to penetrate the container and create algae in the nutrient-rich water. Tinfoil is perfect for this. Avoid using black spray paint is it will heat the water in the box.

Alternative with a bottle

If you want an even easier method, you can use a plastic bottle and cut off the top. Flip the top of the bottle inside the base and place the wicking rope together with the wicking grow media inside. You can choose to leave the cap on and drill a hole in it or remove the cap entirely. You need to keep an eye on the reservoir as it will drain quickly.

Wick system disadvantages

The supply of the plants the wick is not as valid as with other hydroponic systems. The wick can become obstructed by mineral deposits. The problem of this system is that no extra oxygen is supplied to the roots. The system is technically simple, but plant growth is slower compared to other active hydroponic systems.

4.7 Ebb and Flow

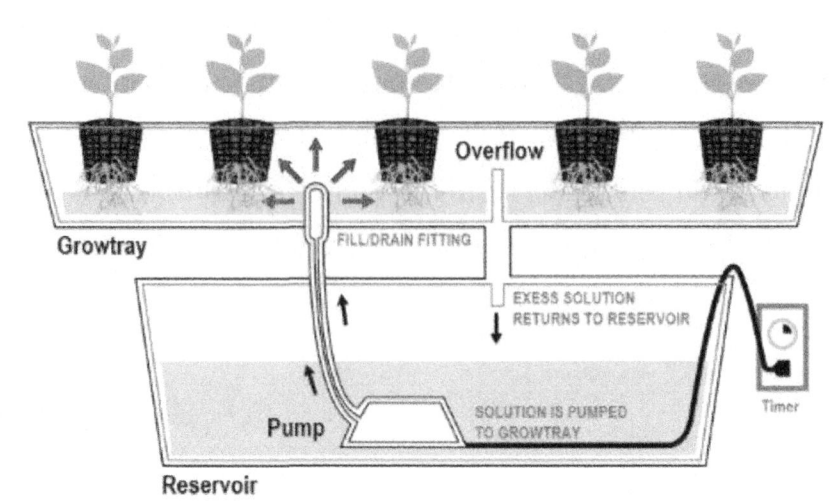

EBB & FLOW CYCLE (PUMP ON)

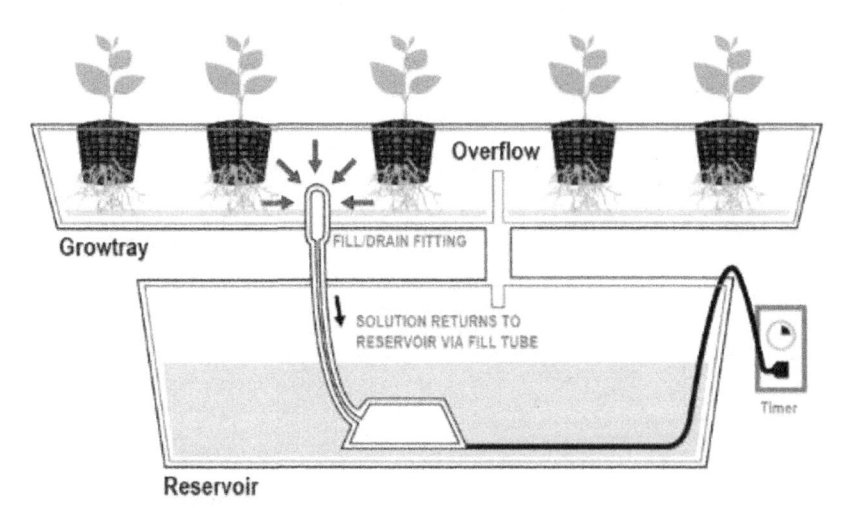

EBB & FLOW CYCLE (PUMP OFF)

This is another system that's easy to set up, and it is mostly used for starting seeds.

As your experience with Hydroponics grows, you'll probably continue to start seeds with this system and then transplant them to a different setup. Commercial farms use this technique for their seedlings.

The Ebb and Flow system work by flooding, for a short time, the tray containing the substrate with a nutrient solution and then sending it back into the tank.

This action usually takes place with a submersible pump connected to a timer.

When the timer turns on the pump, the nutrient solution is pumped into the growth tray. When the timer switches off, the nutrient solution pump flows back into the tank.

The timer is set to switch on several times a day, depending on the size and type of plants, temperature, humidity, and the kind of substrate used.

Ebb and flow system works with a variety of substrates. The interior of the growth tray can be filled with cultivation rocks, gravel, or flaky Rockwool. Many people like to use individual pots full of a substrate. This makes it easier to move plants around or even move them in or out of the system.

The main disadvantage of this type of system is that some kinds of culture mediums (gravel, Growrocks, Perlite) can create multiple drawbacks, such as power outages and pump or timer faults. In that case, the roots can dry out quickly if the irrigation cycles are interrupted.

This problem can be alleviated by using cultivation substrates that retain more water, such as Rockwool, vermiculite, or coconut fiber.

Building your Ebb and Flow System

Here that you'll need:

- a container for your plants

- a water reservoir

- a pump, preferably submersible

- a timer for the pump

- tubing for the pump

- a siphon of your choice

- your choice of growing medium

Start by drilling two holes in the base of your plant container. One hole is for the water to be delivered to the tray; the other will act as an overflow.

Add your water and nutrients to the water container and turn on your pump. You can time how long it takes to fill the plant container until it overflows.

When you shut the pump off, the water will drain back down through the pump pipe and into the water container, creating the ebb and flow.

Probably the sunlight or artificial light will get to the water in the flood and drain tray, and you will need to clean out algae regularly to ensure it isn't using the nutrients and dissolved oxygen meant for the plants.

4.8 Drip system

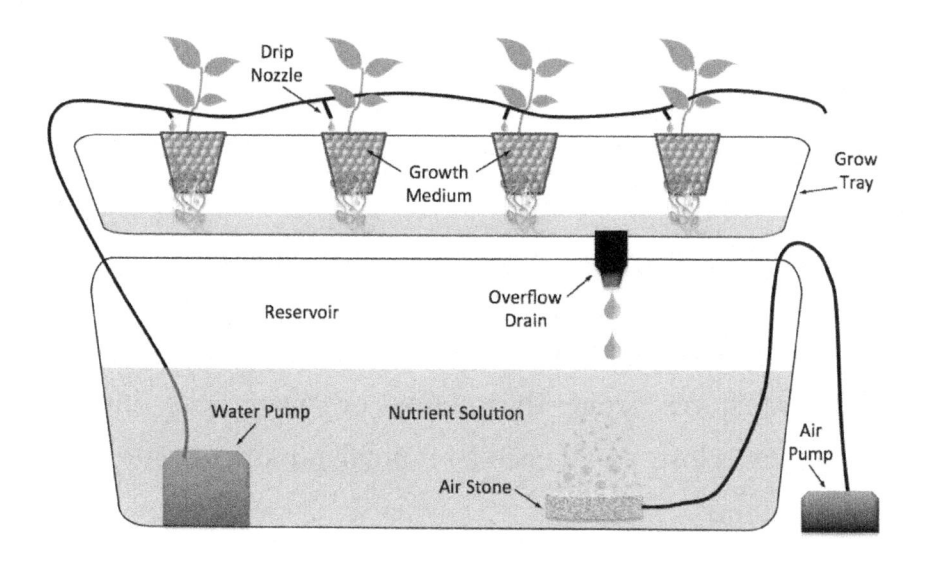

You may have already come across a drip system with conventional soil-potted plants. This is a popular option because it is elementary to add or remove plants and automate the system.

The principle behind this type of hydroponics system is to get the nutrient-rich water to the roots, by dripping it slowly onto the plant roots.

There are two methods of drip systems:

-recirculating

-non-recirculating

Most drip systems are designed as recirculating. A recirculating system pumps the water from the reservoir to the plants. It has a drainage system that allows the water to drain back into the reservoir, effectively allowing the water to go in a circle.

This is an efficient approach as water loss is minimized, only that which transpires from the plants or evaporates into the atmosphere is lost. You'll need a minimal amount of water to top up the system.

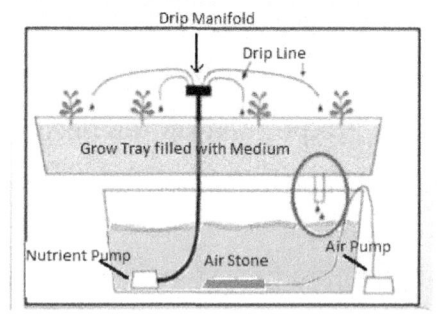

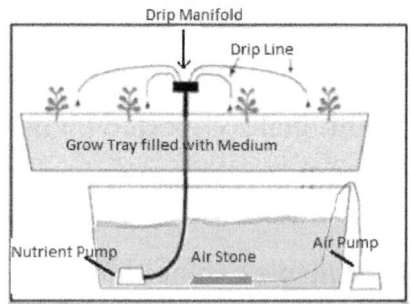

In contrast, the non-recirculating system doesn't allow the water to return to the reservoir. This is why they are also known as "run to waste" systems.

This may seem like a wasteful option as the water will need to be replenished regularly. However, this is a very popular option for commercial farmers because the costs involved are low.

The non-recirculating system is run with a top-up reservoir. The delivery of nutrient-rich water is carefully measured, so no water and nutrients are lost. This minimizes waste.

You will have to mix another batch with a predetermined ratio of nutrients and water. This makes the non-recirculating system easy to operate.

4.9 Vertical system

The vertical hydroponics system is a great space saver and can be made in many different forms. The vertical A system uses NFT channels for the plants while the vertical towers use custom grow towers or three-inch PVC pipes. Both use drip irrigation.

The A-frame hydroponic system is an excellent example of how to create a vertical garden that maximizes the number of plants that can develop in a small space without the need for soil.

This is something that could be done on a small scale, making it ideal for those who want to grow their food but lack the space to do it. Or it could easily be scaled up to a much larger system.

53

Another option worth considering is hydroponic towers.

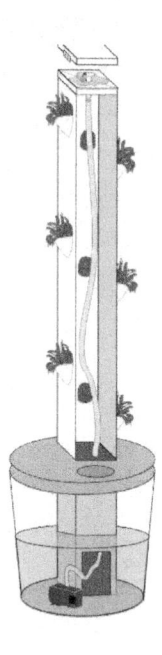

These hydroponic systems for vertical cultivation are ideal for those who have little space and do not have the opportunity to carve out a space for the creation of a traditional horizontal vegetable garden.

Directly related to your budget and the space you have available, you can decide how many towers you want.

A seven-foot tube has slots for approximately twenty plants. Therefore, if you start with six tubes, you will have enough space to grow one hundred and twenty plants.

The water will be supplied to the top of the grow towers and will drip into a collection gutter back to the reservoir.

These towers can be placed in a small greenhouse, in a garden, in a garage, or even in a small room in the house; more and more people are turning to vertical crops, both to experiment with new types of agriculture and for space needs.

4.10 Fogponics

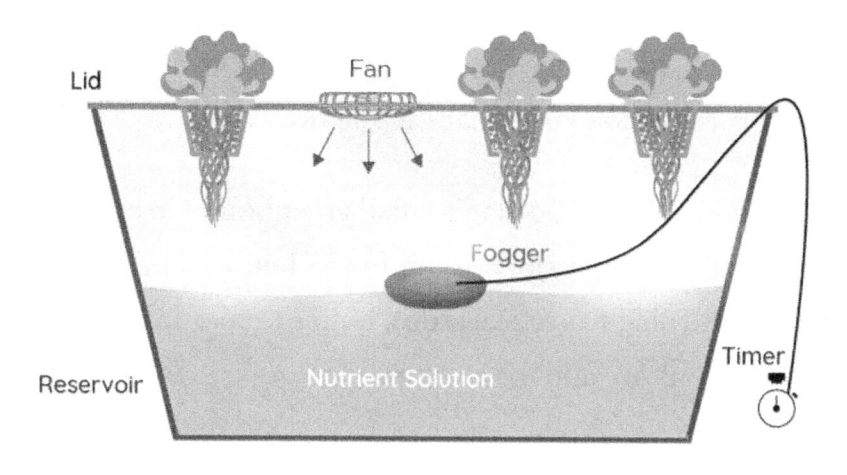

Fogponics works similarly to Aeroponics (that we'll talk about later in the book) but is an advanced form of these because this type of system uses fog instead of misting as the primary growing environment.

It is mainly used to create clones. The fog is created by an ultrasonic device that floats on the water. The vibration evaporates the water.

Fogponics or fog, and ponics (labor) can be defined as working fog. In its most straightforward meaning, in the Fogponics system, growers use the fog to grow plants.

The Fogponic method uses electric nebulizers to pump and vibrate. The combination of water and nutrients turns into humidity. The roots of the plants are, therefore, systematically enveloped by the humid and nutrient-filled mist that is created.

With this cultivation method, the tiny mist particles disperse and spread and completely impregnate the roots of the plants. Plants absorb all the nutrients they need together with moisture and oxygen, just like in all the active hydroponic cultivation methods we've talked about so far.

They don't have to "worry" about finding them in the ground, and therefore, every effort is made to grow, blossom, and germinate if it is a question of seedlings; in case we are producing clones, to root development.

There is a difference with the usual hydroponic systems: instead of taking oxygen from the water (in which an air pump is active), plants are suspended in the air.

In this way, their roots are easily wrapped in oxygen. Nebulizers supply water to plants, and a timer usually automates the action.

Fogponics operates just like Aeroponics. But are used the foggers instead of the water mist. They produce and atomize much smaller droplets than in Aeroponics, usually less than 10 microns in size.

In Fogponics, which plants are better?

Although, in principle, with Fogponics, we can grow all plants, it is advisable to focus on suitable plants to obtain the best results.

Seedling, clonings

The Fogponics system works very well with small plants and cloning. The little clones that have just been obtained from a cutting have poorly developed roots, and it is therefore rather difficult to make them absorb nutrients and keep them hydrated. At the same time, we should not exaggerate the amount of water; too much could excessively load the cloning, too little on the contrary will not give birth to the shoots or dry the roots.

The growers make available to their small clones a set of nutrients and humidity at controlled quantities through the fog produced in the Fogponics system.

Green vegs

The Fogponics also works best with green vegs, including lettuces, spinaches, kales, cucumbers, and beans.

Herbs

Most herbs like basil, mint, and chives thrive in the Fogponic system as it is lightweight, and have a short growing life span.

Advantages of Fogponics system

- Tiny sized droplets. The small droplets tend not to impinge on roots. The cuttings and little seedlings are very delicate and weak; the low-pressure fog does not harm them; that's why Fogponics works so well with cloning.

- High nutrient concentration. The high density of nutrients remains constant inside the tank.

- Easy to clean

Disadvantages of Fogponics system

- Heating produced by the atomizer

The atomizer will be turned on non-stop and can, therefore, increase the temperature inside the tank. The high temperature will evaporate the fog, and the roots can dry out. It will, therefore, be advisable to lower the temperature by programming a timer that will turn the foggers on and off. There is an alternative method: you can add ices. Or buy a water chiller.

- Built-up salt

Over time, the salt will accumulate in the system, and this will block the foggers. It will, therefore, be necessary to clean the system regularly. You can use a toothbrush or soak them all in vinegar. This will ensure that fogponics will always work best.

- Susceptible to a power outage

The whole Fogponics system works thanks to electricity. And the roots are not immersed in water, as in other hydroponic methods, but hung freely. If electricity is missing, the fog stops. All our plants will not be able to absorb the necessary moisture and nutrients; they will dry out quickly and could die.

- High initial cost

This advanced form of Hydroponics will cost you some start-up costs in the beginning.

4.11 Conclusions

There is, therefore, no perfect system or better than others, depending on their needs and experience, each grower will find one system more functional than another.

It is essential to carefully evaluate the various aspects that can influence the choice of the system and to fully understand which technique will be able to best express the potential of your hydroponic garden.

Chapter 5

STARTING CULTIVATION WITH HYDROPONIC TECHNIQUE

5.1 Necessary to Start Hydroponic Cultivation

Here the tools needed in the three germination, growth and final flowering stages

For the Germination Phase:

Necessary:

-Greenhouse (in which to germinate the seeds)

-Rockwool rock wool cubes (at least 1 for each seed to be germinated)

-Root Stimulator

Optional:

-Neon light

-Watertight heating resistance (allows to keep the temperature of the greenhouse stable at the optimal temperature of about 26 degrees)

For the growth and flowering phase:

Necessary:

-Indoor Lighting Kit (in chapter 5.4 we will explain how to choose the lighting system)

-Bulb / bulb

-Power supply

-Lamp / Reflector Holder

-Hydroponic system

-Expanded clay

-pH Tester

-EC Tester

-PH corrector

-Nourishments for the growth phase

-Nourishments for the flowering phase

-Timer for timing

Optional:

-Thermometer/hygrometer

-Grow box / Grow Room or Mylar tent

-Hop on and off (easy roller)

-Humidifier

-Cooling fan

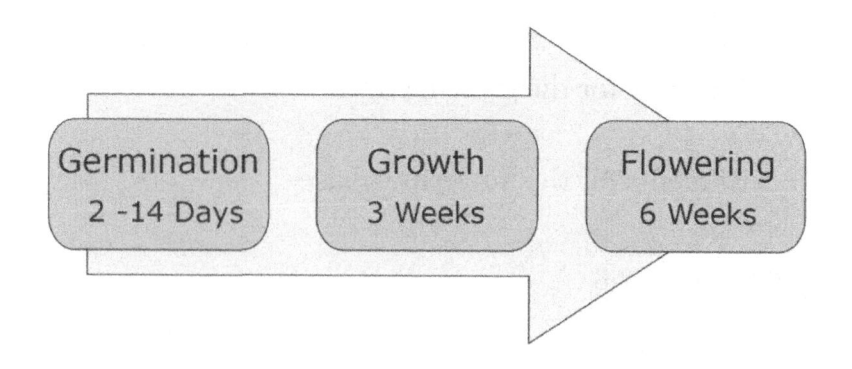

```
[ Germination ]  →  [ Growth ]  →  [ Flowering ]
   2 -14 Days         3 Weeks         6 Weeks
```

Indicative costs to be faced with starting Hydroponic cultivation at home or in a greenhouse

Establishing the final and exact cost of a plant dedicated to hydroponic cultivation is not that simple, because there are a series of variables that affect the ultimate price. However, it is possible to have a general idea to be able to orient yourself. For a private individual who wishes to start hydroponic cultivation at home, the cost to be incurred - for a basic starter kit - ranges between $450 and $550. At the same time, if you want a more complex system, using the latest products and highly technological products in terms of lamps, boxes, and extractors, it can reach $1.100/$1.200.

For those who wish, however, to start real hydroponic agriculture at a professional level, the costs vary significantly, due to a higher number of factors to consider in setting up the system.

Even in this case, however, it is possible to give an idea: it ranges from a minimum of $200 up to a maximum of $1.000, but of course, it is necessary to consider that these are indicative price ranges and that - in any case - the more the area of the cultivated greenhouse increases, the more the average cost will drop.

5.2 Preparation of the germination area

Prepare the rock wool cubes for germination

To prepare the germination area, it is necessary to have rock wool cubes and the root booster to develop the root system of the plants quickly. Below we illustrate the procedure to start the seed germination phase.

- Prepare a solution with 5 liters of water and 20 ml of root stimulator.

- Take the Rockwool cubes and leave them to soak for about 24 hours in the solution of water and Rootbooster to make the Rockwool cubes less alkaline (their pH tends to 7.0).

- The next day drains the cubes. Rockwool cubes retain a lot of water, so it is useful to drain the Rockwool cube to allow a correct exchange of water and oxygen.

- Insert the seed into the hole of the Rockwool cube at a depth of 1/2 (half) cm.

- Insert the cubes inside the mini-greenhouse and keep the temperature at about 79 °F (26 °C) with a high humidity rate (about 80%).

- Move the neon lamp closer and keep it on 24 hours a day.

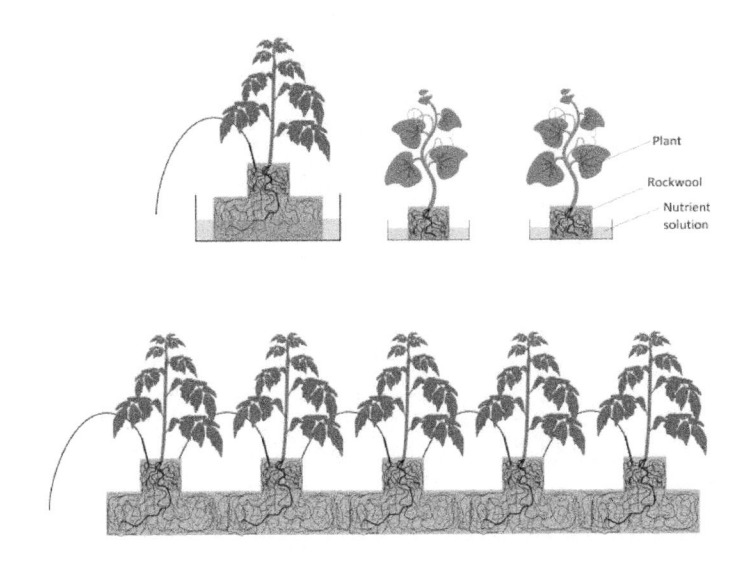

The seed does not initially need light. Once the seedling comes out of the Rockwool cube, however, it is essential to light it with delicate light (preferably neon) or HPS and/or MH lamp (monitoring temperature and humidity).

Seedlings that do not receive adequate light tend to have a very long stem. Depending on the type, quality, and age of the seeds, germination can take from 2 to 14 days.

The roots once crossed the Rockwool cube will tend to come out from the sides and from the bottom of the cube itself

N.B.: the seed in the germination phase is very delicate and must not be touched.

5.3 Installation of the Hydroponic System and Sprout Housing

Once the seed has germinated, it is necessary to plan the preparation of the hydroponic system to plant the rock wool cube.

But how does the hydroponic system work?

In fact, it is good to specify that there are many hydroponic systems on the market, with different characteristics.

In our example, we will use the Atami Wilma Large 4-bowl hydroponic system, which is one of the best-selling with a technology proven by historical results and now guaranteed.

If you decide to use other methods, you should always refer to the instruction manual provided by the manufacturer.

How does a Hydroponic system work and how to set it up?

Here is what we must foresee and prepare and how it is appropriate to set up - in detail - the hydroponic system.

-prepare the lower tank;

-place the pump in the tank;

-house the upper tank;

-place the vases on the upper tank;

-connect the pump to the main fitting;

-connect the main pipe to the drippers and support rods;

-fill the expanded clay pots (remember to wash the clay thoroughly to eliminate dust and impurities)

-connect the pump to the timer and to the power supply (in chapter 5.6 we will deal with the timing of the hydroponic system);

-fill the tank with water and fertilizers (in section 5.11 we will deal in-depth with this topic)

-house the rock wool cube containing the sprout inside the vase containing the expanded clay and house the drippers so that they supply water directly on the cube.

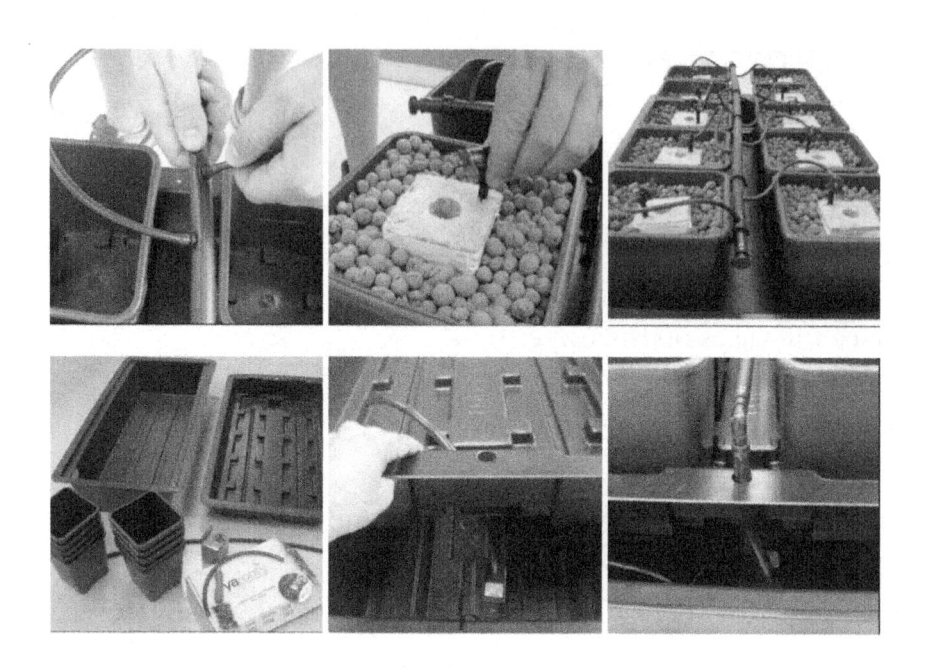

5.4 The lighting system

Once the cubes containing the sprouts have been placed inside the hydroponic system, we must begin to illuminate the seedling (and this applies both to indoor cultivation in the ground, both for hydroponic cultivation, and obviously for aeroponics). To do this, we must prepare a suitable lighting system capable of making the sprout grow and flourish by simulating the effect of sunlight.

A lighting system for hydroponics and indoors is composed of the following elements:

Power supply (or Ballast)

It is used to provide a discharge of current sufficient to turn on the lamp. There are two types of power supplies on the market, the iron-magnetic and the electronic ones.

Electronic ballasts have the advantage over ferromagnetic ballasts of:

-consume less electricity;

-to heat very little;

-to be more stable and therefore increase the life of the bulb;

-wiring is more straightforward because they have the connection to the electrical network already wired;

-some models (dimmable) can adjust the watts and, therefore, to manage bulbs of different wattage.

Hydroponic lamp: what is it?

The lamp that in indoor and hydroponic cultivation provides a specific light spectrum to simulate the effect of the sun.

We often speak of a hydroponic lamp, but - in reality - it is more appropriate to speak of a specific bulb or bulb for hydroponic cultivation, which - thanks to the particular spectrum of light - simulates and reproduces the effects and benefits of sunlight. There are various types of bulbs on the market dedicated to indoor cultivation. The difference lies in the kind of technology and the different background of light and colors. For growth, a blue light spectrum is suggested.

For the flowering phase, however, an illumination spectrum tending towards orange/red is indicated. Agro lamps are usable during the growth and flowering periods, while MH is usable only during the vegetative phase (when the plant grows) while HPS is for the flowering stage.

The choice between Agro and MH - HPS: Agro bulbs are certainly a more comfortable and economical solution than MH and HPS bulbs since they are used throughout the life cycle of the plant.

Agro lamps have the disadvantage of having a lower yield during the growth phase compared to MH.

Lamp holder / Reflector

It is used to accommodate the bulb and spread the light distribution in the cultivation area.

Also, in this case, there are many models on the market and properties. We can say, however, that there are two basic types of reflectors, air-cooled reflectors and those that are not. The latter has the advantage of being designed in such a way as to allow forced air passage from an extractor that can cool the heat emitted by the bulb, effectively preventing the temperature from rising inside the grow room.

Choose the size of the indoor and hydroponic lighting system

The diagram below helps you to define the size of the lighting system, starting from the available space and the number of plants you wish to grow. The size of the grow box (optional) to be associated with the type of lighting system is also indicated for convenience.

Warning! Always remember that the power supply and the bulb must have the same wattage

	150 watt	250 watt	400 watt	600 watt	1.000 watt
number of plants	1/2	2/4	3/6	4/10	8/18
Square meters	0,5	0,75	1	1,4	1,5
Grow Room Box	32"x32"x72" 70x70x180 cm	36"x36"x72" 80x80x180 cm	39"x39"x80" 100x100x200 cm	48"x48"x80" 120x120x200 cm	96"x48"x80" 240x120x200 cm

Lighting system wiring:

1. Connect the power supply to the mains *

There are various types of power supplies on the market.

Some are simpler to wire such as electronic ballasts because they already have a connection to the electricity grid ready, others like ferromagnetic ones are more complex

2. Connect the power supply to the lamp/reflector holder *

3. The current from the power supply must be brought and connected to the lamp holder to which the lamp is screwed and then powered.

The lamp holder for these types of uses always has a standard attachment called E40.

4. The lamp/reflector holder: It has the function of reflecting and diffusing the light produced by the lamp. Generally, it is supplied complete with a lamp holder.

There are various shapes and sizes on the market. It is often provided with protective plastics, so it is good to be careful and remove them before putting it into operation.

5. Screw the bulb to the bulb holder *.

6. Once everything is wired, screw the bulb to the lamp holder until it stops. Clean the bulb with a cloth before turning it on.

* Refer to the manuals and instructions provided by the manufacturer for the connections between the parts.

5.5 Set up the Grow Room

The optimal environmental conditions in which to set up the cultivation area

A grow room is a growing area for indoor growing. It is possible to grow indoors in any closed space. However, it is necessary to take into account several factors to ensure that all the parameters useful for the growth of the plant are regularly monitored and controlled to obtain the best possible result.

Below we can list the essential elements to manage in the cultivation area (grow room):

1. The light

2. The temperature

3. Humidity

4. Aeration, ventilation and carbon dioxide (CO_2)

In the following chapters, we will deal in-depth with each of these points and analyze the solutions to the most common problems that occur when the threshold values of each parameter are exceeded.

In the image, you will find an illustration of all the components useful for managing vital signs in a grow room.

GROW ROOM SETUP

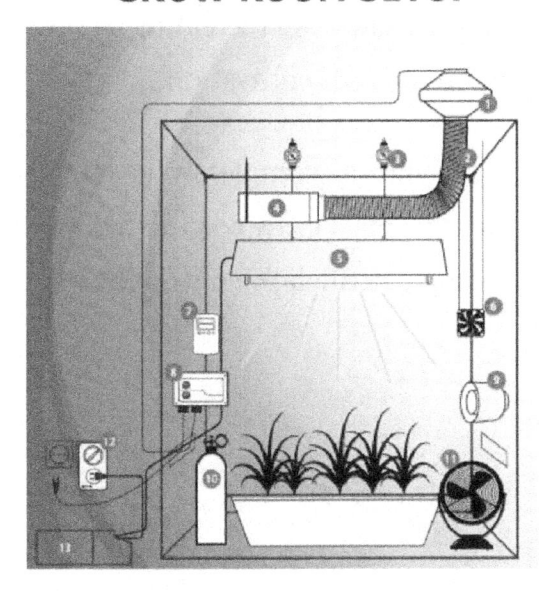

1) Air extractor
   Needed to control temperature and humidity

2) Flexible conduct
   Connect the extractor to the carbon filter

3) Easy Roller
   Pulleys to adjust the height of the lamp

4) Activated carbon filter
   Filters the air exiting the air extractor making it odor-free

5) Lamp

6) Axial fan
   Eliminates "hotspot" produced by the lamp

7) Hygrometer
   Measures the values of min/max temperature and humidity

8) Climate control unit
   Connected to the extractor, it manages the temperature and humidity

9) Axial extractor
   Introduces air flow

10) Co2 cylinder

11) Cooling fan
    Avoids stagnation of air in the cultivation environment

12) Analog timer
    Daily timer to manage the light

13) Hps Mh power supply
    Able to turn on bulbs Hps, Mh and Agro

5.6 The Light in the Grow Room

Light in indoor cultivation is an essential element. Plants will need to receive the right amount of light from recreating the cycle that naturally provides the sun in outdoor cultivation.

In indoor cultivation, it is advisable to completely isolate the cultivation area, perhaps by purchasing a grow box that prevents access to natural light so that we can artificially control the hours of light and dark.

Another advantage of the ready-made grow rooms that can be purchased on the market is that they are lined with reflective material, which guarantees complete reflexivity, which allows better light diffusion. If a grow room is not used, it is possible to cover the cultivation area with reflective sheets.

Light hours in the growth and flowering stages

During the growth phase, it is necessary to provide the plant with about 18 hours of light per day.

In the third or fourth week of the growth phase, it is possible to reduce the hours of light from 18 to 12. The plant will perceive the arrival of autumn (effect: "shorter days"), then it will begin to bloom before winter arrives.

In any case, it is not recommended to make the plant bloom when it is still too small and weak since it would not be able to support many flowers.

Using the timer to control the switching on and off of the lights

The timer is handy for regulating the switching on and off of the lights. There are several types on the market; the cheapest ones are the analog timers that provide programming in 24 hours in general in a 15-minute passage.

The digital timers are set to multiple programming and arranged to set up to 20 different programs. Finally, there are timers and multiple channels that lend light to the various power outlets.

5.7 Temperature in the Grow Room

The tools to control and regulate the temperature in Hydroponic cultivation

In all indoor and outdoor cultivations, regardless of the type of soil or substrate used and the type of systems used to grow plants, temperature plays a fundamental role in the success of cultivation, even in indoor ones with a hydroponic system. For this reason, it is one of the parameters to be monitored continuously and adjusted, to make sure that it is always in the preset and therefore optimal parameters, which oscillate between 70°F (21°C) and 82°F (28°C) degrees centigrade. If the temperature rises above 82°F (28°C) or drops below 70°F (21°C), it could cause severe damage to your plants.

To prevent this from happening, it is essential to monitor using specific measuring instruments, i.e., thermometers and thermo-hygrometers.

The recommendation is to buy a digital thermometer that allows you to correctly and accurately check the temperature of the grow room or hydroponic cultivation environment, at any time of the day, including monitoring and recording the minimum and maximum temperature reached during an arc of time.

Only in this way can we notice if the temperature has exceeded the recommended parameters and avoid problems that could be more or less serious.

But what should be done if the temperature rises or falls compared to the recommended values? How is it possible to run for cover?

To lower the temperature in the grow room of your hydroponic cultivation, it is possible to use an aspirator or air extractor, which sucks in and extracts the hot air, gradually lowering the room temperature. If the rise in temperature should occur often, it is possible to provide a thermostat programmed to activate the extractor only during the hot hours, when the indoor lights are on. If the temperature does not drop even with the extractor, an air conditioner can be used to lower it.

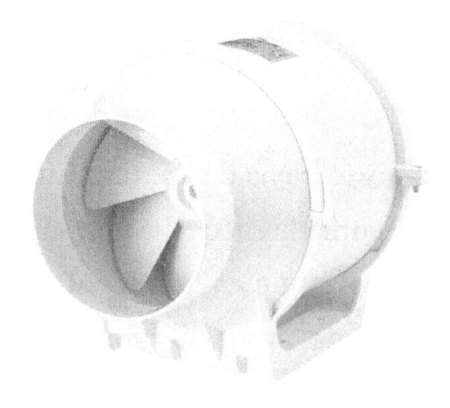

If, on the contrary, the temperature of indoor cultivation with hydroponic system should be too low, below 21 degrees centigrade, it is possible - even in this case - to use a thermostat, which can activate a stove capable of heating the environment and raise the temperature by a few degrees, especially when the lights are off.

5.8 Grow Room moisture

Humidity is another fundamental parameter to be kept under control in the indoor cultivation area. The ideal humidity for indoor growing is around 50-60%. The hygrometer is the measuring instrument to monitor the percentage of humidity present in the grow room. When the humidity is too high, it causes molds to arise, which results in the progressive deterioration of the plant.

What to do if the humidity is too high:

To decrease the humidity in the grow room, an air extractor is sufficient as for the temperature. The suction of hot and humid air allows a lowering of humidity.

What to do if the humidity is too low:

When the humidity is too low, a humidifier is sufficient for a grow room.

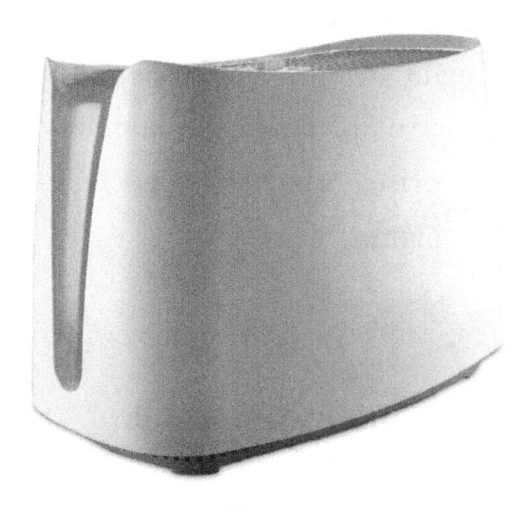

5.9 The Ventilation of the Grow Room

Proper ventilation allows our cultivation air to avoid humidity accumulation and temperature rise.

The ventilation in the grow room, and in general, the air circulation is a factor of primary importance. As previously seen, proper ventilation allows our cultivation air to avoid the accumulation of humidity and raising the temperature.

The air extraction process, therefore, becomes an indispensable element whose goal is the extraction of internal air so that all the air is extracted every 4/6 minutes. An extraction system consists of the following items:

1. The extractor to suck the air

2. The duct or extraction hose

3. The fan for the intake of fresh air

4. A fan (optional to improve air recirculation)

5. An activated carbon filter (optional to eliminate odors at the outlet)

Selection and sizing of the ventilation system.

An air extractor must be chosen above all based on the flow rate. To calculate it, multiply the volume of the grow room (or grow box) by 75. To choose the appropriate extractor, do this calculation:

Height x Width x Depth x 75 = Air extractor flow rate.

Once the extractor flow rate has been calculated, we can choose a suitable model. Once the model and its diameter have been selected, the pipes must be purchased, paying attention to respect their diameter or choosing the necessary reducers.

To join the extractor to the pipe/duct, use jointing bands or resistant scotch tape.

It is possible to automate the ventilation circuit through special control units which have the function of regulating the extractor power when parameters (temperature and humidity) vary.

Carbon dioxide (CO2) in the Grow Room

When growing in an enclosed environment, there is a risk that the growing plants consume a lot of carbon dioxide (CO2); if this occurs, the growth of the plant will slow down significantly.

To maintain high levels of Co2, it will be sufficient to let outside air into the grow room through an extractor. Often, however, excessive air circulation causes the temperature to drop excessively. In this case, we can forcefully dispense carbon dioxide through a CO2 bottle dispenser.

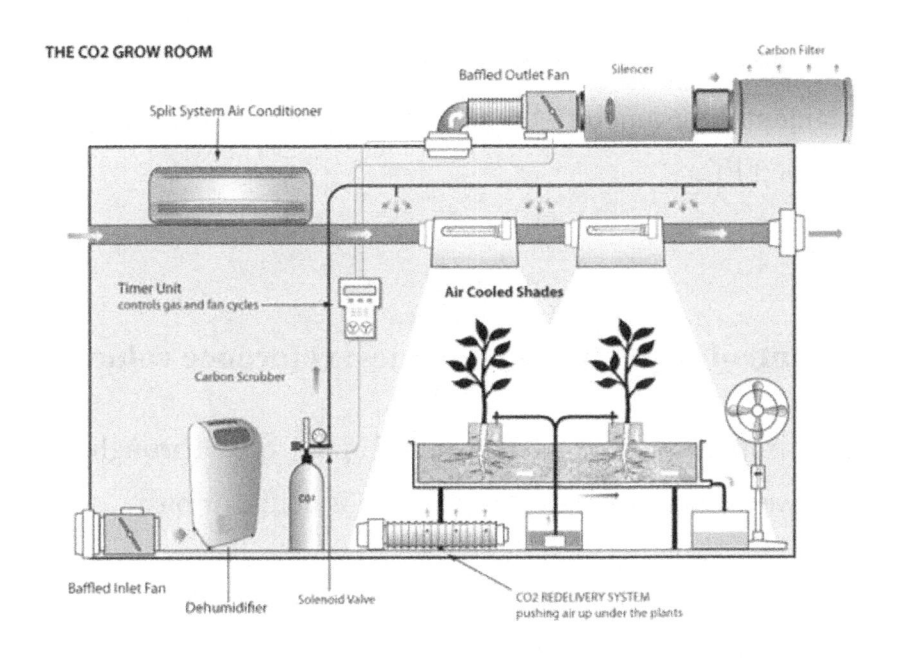

5.10 Water Quality in Hydroponic: PH, EC, and Temperature

Control, increase and decrease of the water values in the Hydroponic system

Hydroponic irrigation of plants is vital because through irrigation - in addition to providing water - all the nutrients the plant needs are also administered.

In hydroponics, water is a much more relevant and vital factor than land cultivation. We must pay close attention to two fundamental parameters the pH and the electrical conductivity, also called EC.

The control of pH in Hydroponics: reference values

The hydroponic pH must be around 5.8 - 6.0. Through a pH meter, we can determine if the solution is acidic or basic.

The optimal pH in hydroponics must be around 5.8 - 6.0.

What to do if the pH is too high or too low?

If the solution is too acidic, it will be sufficient to correct it by increasing the pH (pH +), if the water is too basic, we will fix it by decreasing the pH (pH-).

pH- Contains 30% phosphoric acid to reduce the pH value of the nutrient solution.

pH + Contains potassium carbonate to increase the PH value during the growth and flowering phase.

Nutrient Availability & ph

Electrical conductivity control - EC

Electrical or EC conductivity is measured in mS/sec milli-Siemens per second through a conductivity meter. Measuring the EC is used to establish the quantity of salts dissolved in the water.

The salts naturally present in the water of the water network can vary from area to area so often if we are in areas with a high concentration of salts it is preferable to use osmotic water or water that has been previously filtered through a reverse osmosis system that leads to values of water conductivity close to zero.

The recommended electrical conductivity - EC values vary according to the germination and growth / flowering phase

In the germination phase, the Ec must be between a minimum of 0.6 and a maximum of 1.0.

In the growth and flowering phases, the Ec must be between a minimum of 1.0 and a maximum of 2.0.

In the last flowering phase, it is advisable to drop again between a minimum of 0.6 and a maximum of 1.0.

How to adjust the water EC: what to do if the electrical conductivity EC is too high or too low?

When the EC is too low, it is sufficient to increase the amount of fertilizer, while if it is too high, we must decrease the fertilizer.

The water temperature: reference values

The water temperature is critical in hydroponics. In hydroponics, the temperature must be between a minimum of 59°F (15°C) and a maximum of 73°F (23°C).

What to do if the water temperature is too high or too low?

When you introduce new water into the system, pay attention to the starting temperature, and if it is too cold, it is essential to wait until it warms up to room temperature. When the water temperature is too low in production, the ambient temperature is probably also too low. And the same principle applies in the case of too high temperatures. Therefore, before proceeding to raise or lower the water temperature directly, act, and adjust the temperature of the external environment.

5.11 Fertilization of Hydroponics

Fertilizers and nutrients are for plants like food for humans

Fertilizers and nutrients are for plants such as food for humans and are, therefore, a fundamental element in indoor cultivation. There are many types on the market with different characteristics. Still, it is crucial to make sure the fertilizer used is suitable for the kind of cultivation we are carrying out. For example, if we grow in hydroponics, we must use a specific fertilizer for hydroponic cultivation, which will be composed of specific elements suitable on inert substrates such as clay or rock wool.

All fertilizer manufacturers supply the so-called fertigation schemes which are used to synthesize the products and quantities to be administered in the weeks of the plant life cycle. It is advisable to refer to the manufacturer's indications for times and doses of administration.

Organic and Mineral Fertilizers: which to choose and why

Fertilizers provide plants with all the macroelements (Nitrogen, Phosphorus, Potassium) and microelements they need to grow properly and healthily.

Both organic and mineral fertilizers provide plants with the main macroelements for their development. So what are the main differences between the two types of fertilizers?

Organic or Mineral: the release method

The main difference between mineral and organic fertilizers lies in how the elements are released and how they are absorbed by the plants through the soil.

Organic fertilizers - among which we can include guano, manure, dried blood, and bone meal - slowly degrade and are assimilated by plants within weeks or months, unlike mineral ones that break up immediately, and they are readily assimilable.

Which to choose?

Organic fertilizers are indeed indicated for the preparation of the seedbed and for an annual and more natural fertilization (they do not contain chemical impurities). In contrast, mineral fertilizers can be used in the vegetative and productive phase of plants. It is important to underline how the two types of fertilizers are not mutually exclusive, but instead can be used in a complementary way.

But beware of excess fertilization

Whether they are organic or mineral, excess fertilization must always be avoided: an excessive dose can, in fact, irreparably damage the plant and its healthy growth. It is therefore recommended always to respect the doses indicated in the bottle, and in case of excess fertilization, rinse the earth promptly with plenty of water at room temperature.

Chapter 6

BEST PLANTS FOR HYDROPONICS

Plants suitable for Hydroculture

First of all, it is necessary to know that cuttings rooted in water are ideal for starting hydroculture because, for them, it is much easier to adapt to the expanded clay substrate since it is mainly composed of water.

If you want to start with the cultivation of hydroculture plants, there is a great variety to choose from. If you are a lover of aromatic herbs, the rosemary plant is perfect for growing in hydroculture if you start from cutting; otherwise, you can choose other types of ornamental and very decorative plants, such as Ficus, Calathea, Pothos, Dracena, and Philodendron.

All plants characterized by leaves of tropical origin are well suited to hydroculture, such as the orchid and all those species that present a rapid development to the root system.

And what about flowering plants? In these cases, the most recommended species for home hydroculture are Hibiscus, Spathiphyllum, Kalanchoe, Anthurium, or Saintpaulia. Still, nothing prevents you from trying to cultivate other types of plants as well.

What about succulents? Succulents have a more complicated situation since they do not tolerate excess humidity. Therefore the recommended species for hydroculture are aloe, succulent plants, and - as anticipated above - orchids.

6.1 Lettuce

Growing salad in hydroponics is elementary, much more than it might seem, even for those who start from scratch and approach the hydroponics world for the first time.

Once you have identified the variety of salad that best suits your needs and tastes, you must obtain the seeds that you will easily find online. Then you will have to buy rock wool cubes (Rockwool) and net jars, a mini-green to store them in the warm, in a protected environment and with net pots, designed precisely for the needs of plants that are grown with hydroponic and aeroponic systems. Therefore, a small hydroponic or aeroponic system will be needed.

The salad seeds must be placed inside the moistened rock wool cubes (it is recommended not to insert more than five seeds for each cube) only with water and then placed inside the mini-greenhouse, at a temperature that can oscillate between 73°F (23°C) and 82°F (28°C).

One aspect to check - when using rock wool cubes - is the amount of water they absorb, because an excessive amount of liquid could cause the roots to rot and drown them. For this, it is always advisable to check the liquid levels present and possibly wring out the cubes to let out the excess water.

With the right amount of water and the ideal temperature, lettuce seeds will begin to germinate after about 48 hours. When you see the first roots appearing from the rock wool cubes (both from the sides and the base), it means that the time has come to transfer the newly born seedlings to the special mesh pots, which will first be filled with expanded clay and then settled in the hydroponic system you have chosen (or aeroponic). The seedlings inserted in the aeroponic system will then be fed with a special nutrient solution based on water and fertilizers to provide everything they need. It is vital to avoid any fertilizer during the germination phase and then start with a halved dose compared to what is recommended on the package.

Fertilizers for the cultivation of Hydroponic salad

By using suitable fertilizers and in the right dose, the roots of the lettuce seedlings are allowed to develop better and faster than they would use with a traditional cultivation system, also because - in this way - the roots can receive and assimilate nutrients faster.

To grow the seedlings in a healthy and fast way, thus strengthening their root system to make it more robust, it is possible to opt for some special fertilizers, which contain fundamental substances capable of promoting and increasing growth, accelerating absorption nutrients, and keep the most common salad diseases away. Fertilizers play a central role in the life and health of the plant. Since the hydroponic and aeroponic system does not provide for the presence of fertile soil, to ensure that the salad receives all the nutrients, it is essential to use the right fertilizers to be able to grow plants properly. Strengthening the root system of salad plants and preventing pests means growing healthy, strong, and vigorous plants capable of returning a good harvest.

Hydroponic salad: parameters to monitor

At this point, once the cultivation has started, it is appropriate to keep under control some fundamental values for the health and growth of each plant, such as the pH, which will determine the ability - by the cultivated plant - to correctly absorb the available nutrients.

In order for salad plants to absorb all nutrients correctly, the pH must be slightly acidic, and to ensure that it is always such, it is advisable to often monitor the situation with manual tests. For example, cheap and easy-to-use paper strips for pH testing can be used.

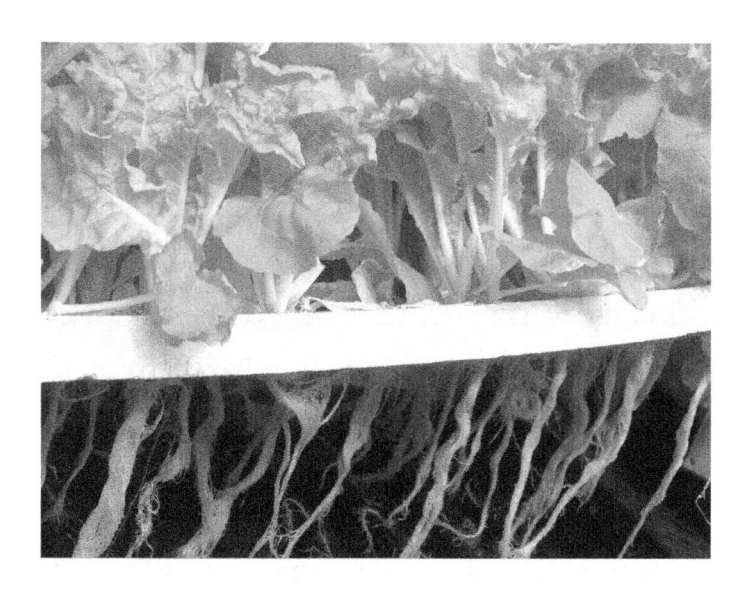

Tips and tricks for a perfect Hydroponic salad

To create a suitable and protected environment, it is recommended to repair and check the salad plants inside a grow box to make them grow well, healthily and faster, without weighing on the cost of the bill.

Among the advantages of using the grow box, there is undoubtedly that of being able to more easily control the temperature than a larger environment and, therefore, less controlled, better manage ventilation, ensure the right lighting (thanks to the reflective mylar sheet present inside the grow box which allows the light to be effectively propagated).

But when will you get your first salad crop?

Much depends on the variety chosen and cultivated, but - in general - it is possible to say that the time required varies between 4 weeks and 80 days. By choosing different varieties and managing the aeroponic system, you can have a fresh, tasty, and healthy salad at any time of the year.

To help grow, salad plants should be adequately lit: the best solution is to use HID discharge lamps or LEDs, but a good compromise can also be found by using fluorescent lamps.

To better manage the lighting of the salad plants, it is advisable to activate the lights for 12 hours a day, thus ensuring 12 hours of darkness.

For beginners, it is advisable to purchase a simple lighting set consisting of 4 CFL lamps, sufficient for home cultivation.

6.2 Strawberries

Cross and delight of many professional and amateur growers, the strawberry is a problematic fruit, especially if grown out of season and in unsuitable environments. All difficulties are overcome, especially for those who choose the above-ground cultivation, better known as hydroponic cultivation.

The more than tested technique, especially in strawberry cultivation, offers more than exciting advantages:

- production is standardized;

- there is a considerable saving of energy and water, which is used more rationally;

- production is better in quality and quantity;

- the problem of diseases, molds, and pests that multiply on contact with the ground are entirely forgotten.

Those who choose the hydroponic technique also have the opportunity to produce strawberries in at least two different periods of the year: from October to December and throughout April and May.

If we also take into consideration that once planted, the plants begin to bear fruit after 45 days. It is well understood why this choice is shared by many growers and lovers of indoor cultivation.

Anyone who chooses to switch to this type of technique must first thoroughly wash the roots of their seedlings and insert them in a small pot that contains expanded clay or alchemy of vermiculite and perlite.

It is also essential to have a container that can hold at least 10 liters of water (for each seedling), better if impermeable to the passage of light to avoid the formation of algae and mushrooms.

Among the most popular hydroponic cultivation methods for strawberries, there is the one called NFT hydroponics: to make it simple with this system; it is possible to achieve a good circulation of all the nutrients that the roots need. Everything is automated thanks to the use of a timer that alternates between full and dry moments, essential for the roots to have the right oxygenation.

Obviously, it is essential to have the right fertilizer, which in this case, is composed of nitrogen and potassium and water with the correct pH, which should always be adjusted between 5.5 and 5.6. To make the job easier, there are active acidity regulators on the market.

Finally, you must have the right lighting, and in this case, the lamps for indoor cultivation will be a potent ally.

Once you start your strawberry cultivation, domestic or industrial, it is good to keep in mind that the plant must be regularly pruned: it is wrong not to cut excess leaves, especially before flowering. These will unnecessarily weaken the plant and could favor the creation of mushrooms that are particularly harmful to the future growth of strawberries.

Also, despite the impatience shared by many growers, it is good that the fruit is harvested only when red and ripe, better still if in times of darkness.

6.3 Tomatoes

Quality and quantity with Hydroponic tomato cultivation

Tomato is a genuinely functional vegetable in hydroponic culture. It reacts very well to the so-called "soilless cultivation," this because it can easily adapt to different types of substrate and does not require demanding agronomic management.

In tomato hydroponics, multiple substrates can be used:

- Rock wool

- Peat

- Perlite

- Coconut fiber

- Compost

And with all, you can achieve magnificent results. The only precaution that must be paid in the hydroponic cultivation of tomatoes is the temperature. Indeed, excessive maxims could affect the floral drop and, therefore, on the quantity and quality of the product.

6.4 Kitchen herbs

The new home dream is to have a thousand and one aromatic herbs on the terrace or the balcony to flavor your dishes with a personal, fresh, and eco-friendly touch. This is why hydroponics has been so successful.

The Greeks already knew it, Francis Bacon spoke about it in 1627 and today hydroponics (literally the art of growing plants in water) is well appreciated in the industrial and domestic field.

The hydroponic cultivation of aromatic herbs has five remarkable qualities:

1. the yield of the product that is developed through indoor cultivation is better;

2. growth is faster;

3. the taste is more intense;

4. the cultivation technique is environmentally sustainable;

5. the water expenditure decreases drastically.

With hydroponic cultivation at home, it is possible to grow any aromatic plant, whether it is parsley, basil, thyme, rosemary, oregano. Still, you can also choose to grow lettuces, tomatoes, strawberries, and who knows what else.

In short, hydroponics allows at reduced costs and with a disarming simplicity to make your terrace or balcony a garden of wonders, a vertical garden, an urban oasis.

The roots of our aromatic seedlings will seek support on an inert substrate often made up of expanded clay, pralines, coconut fiber, or other similar materials. Of course, the irrigation that the plant receives must be rich in inorganic compounds that will be able to give it all the nutrients that generally come from the earth. Your cultivation of aromatic herbs will surely provide unparalleled satisfaction.

6.5 Orchids

Orchids lend themselves perfectly to hydroculture. They are, in fact, epiphytic plants (i.e., plants that naturally grow and live on other plants), and humid environments represent their ideal condition for growing well and in health. The plant will develop its roots, which - with the growth and passage of time - will pass through the holes of the pot, to flow directly into the water. Different varieties of orchids can be grown in hydroculture, such as the best-known variety of Phalaenopsis, but also Cattleya, the Dendrobium variety, Paphiopedilum and Oncidium.

One of the main advantages offered by this cultivation technique is represented by the opportunity to supply the plant with a constant quantity of water capable of properly hydrating and irrigating the orchid without damaging it with an excess of liquid. All this - combined with correct fertilization - allows the plant to grow at a much faster rate than traditional cultivation techniques.

Another advantage of orchids grown in hydroculture is given by the typical characteristics of expanded clay, used in these cases instead of the soil or the mix of materials generally used for orchids, which allows faster, easier, and risk-free repotting to damage the roots.

In this way, orchids quickly develop their root system: in a short time, the roots will grow and pass through the holes of the pot in which they are located and will begin to develop directly in the cultivation water.

By doing so, orchid plants will grow faster and healthier, without any disadvantages.

As already mentioned, there are many benefits of using the hydroculture method:

The plant needs much less maintenance

Faster and faster growth

A reduction in the risk of pests and diseases

Greater oxygenation of the roots

Elimination of mold and other allergens.

6.6 Plants to avoid in Hydroponic cultivation

Some plants are not precisely indicated in hydroponic cultivation. Here are a few:

Pumpkins

Pumpkins love the sun and well-drained soil with neutral pH.

They are challenging to grow in a hydroponic system as they have large groups of roots that spread rapidly.

Squash

Squash grows at the base of the plant, which means it could rest on damp soils. This will likely encourage mushroom growth.

Also, squash is generally a large plant with minimal yield. There are much better ways to use space in the hydroponic system.

Zucchini

This is a great plant, which means it will need a lot of support. It needs more nutrients than other plants and won't give such a significant yield for space.

It is necessary to keep the temperature around 75 ° F (24 ° C), even during the night. It will also dry out very quickly if it does not have enough water and nutrients.

Potatoes

Most root vegetables are not suitable for hydroponic systems. Potatoes are such a case.

The cost of the harvest will be very low compared to the efforts needed to grow it.

Radish

Some plants will grow well, but they are still not a good option. You need the right supports to make them grow hydroponically, and in the end, the cost will probably be higher than buying in a store.

Chapter 7

HYDROPONICS VS AQUAPONICS

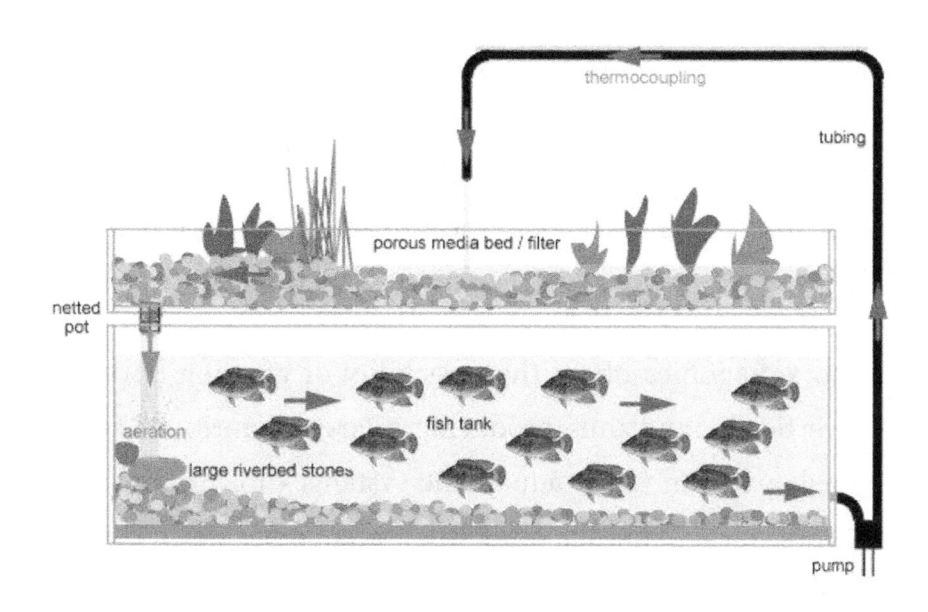

With an aquaponics system, it is possible to use 1/10 of the amount of water generally used for the irrigation of traditional crops in soil: even less water than the quantities used in hydroponic cultivation. Furthermore, being a natural ecosystem, it is not possible to use harmful petrochemical products, pesticides, or herbicides.

To feed it and make it work, feed the fish in the system and collect the plants that will develop.

Among the advantages offered by this type of system, there is undoubtedly great freedom in choosing the place; in fact, it is possible to grow anywhere: at home or in a garage, in a greenhouse, or in a courtyard to be set up as you prefer. But there is more because everything is scalable: based on the available budget, it is possible to choose the size and space to be dedicated to this type of system, which can be expanded even later.

In fact, aquaponics offers the possibility of growing anywhere, even vertically, and thus producing a large quantity of food in minimal space. In tower aquaponic systems - for example - the plants are stacked on each other, the water comes down from the top of the tower and reaches the roots and then falls directly into the fish tank.

Among the ideal cultivation systems for aquaponics, there is undoubtedly the DWC (deep water culture), which provides a large cultivation container, low and wide, which floats in a channel full of water from fish and appropriately filtered to remove the solid waste. The plants are placed in special holes created within the cultivation plan; here, the roots of the plants are free and in contact with the underlying water. This method is ideal for growing salads and other vegetables that grow rapidly and don't need large quantities of nutrients.

Another system widely used in aquaponic cultivation is the TFT (Nutrient film Technique), which provides for the presence of a slightly inclined tank on the bottom of which a mat rich in nutrients is applied.

Inside the tank, water flows, which takes the nutrients from the film placed on the bottom and distributes them to the roots of the plants that directly touch the water flow.

The plants are arranged inside holes made in a tube placed above the inclined tank: in this way, the roots hang freely in this continuous flow of water. This cultivation method works very well for plants that need little support, such as strawberries and broad-leaved vegetables, for example.

The NFT system is also a great way to develop crops vertically and use unused space because it can be hung from the ceiling above other crops.

How does Aquaponics work?

Aquaponics effectively transforms the cultivation plant into a small, completely autonomous ecosystem, in which water is continuously recovered, and waste is recycled from the roots.

The combination of water, fish, and plants represents the ideal opportunity to discover, deepen, and convey the importance of self-sufficiency and sustainability. The aquaponic cultivation system is characterized by a recirculation system, where the water - with the help of suitable pumps - is taken from the tank where the fish are located and conveyed into a filter, which carries out the nitrification process, bringing the formation of nitrite and nitrate destined to be assimilated by plants.

In essence, the water collects and transports all the liquid. Solid waste naturally produced by fish (which without polluting it pollutes the environment), and the system filters them thanks to the help of beneficial bacteria, which transform them into nutrients. At this point, the now purified nutrient solution returns to the plants' disposal, to guarantee them the right nutrients, and then is put back into the fish breeding tank, thus closing the cycle. In this way, the waste is eliminated, and the plants get the right amount of nutrients without the need for additional nutrients.

Which plants can be grown with Aquaponics?

The varieties of plants that can be grown with the aquaponics method are many, potentially all; in particular, all those that do not need specialized supports to grow, including broad-leaved vegetables, salads, courgettes, aubergines, and aromatic herbs.

What fish for Aquaponics?

As for the fish that can be used within an aquaculture system, it is possible to choose any freshwater fish, including prawns. Of course, depending on the type of fish chosen, it is necessary to set the system differently, based on the characteristics of the variety selected, in order to ensure the right amount and type of nutrients for the plants.

What do you need to create an Aquaculture facility?

To build an aquaculture plant from scratch, it is necessary to purchase a tank intended for breeding fish, a hydroponic tank equipped with a pump - which will be positioned above that of the fish - in which plants will be placed, bacteria that allow the decomposition of the waste of the fish, filters, a kit to measure and adjust the pH, supplements to solve any problems and nutritional deficiencies and then, of course, the fish you prefer and the plants to grow.

To start aquaculture with serenity, it is advisable to purchase a system and ready-to-use kits, which will only need to be assembled and set up following the instructions on the package.

In general, the start-up and maintenance of an aquaponic system does not require great care and attention, but - like all crops of this type, including hydroponics and aeroponics - it requires some checks, such as adequate temperature, pH, humidity (here the section dedicated to conductivity meters), correct ventilation and aeration, (here the section dedicated to air extractors), surface cleaning and the right amount of nutrients (therefore correct number of fish).

One of the crucial aspects to consider at the beginning, in fact, is precisely the relationship - which must be well balanced - between the number and type of plants chosen and the number and breed of fish you wish to breed.

In this way, you can guarantee a healthy and efficient environment.

The other factor to always keep in mind is the nourishment provided to the fish, which must be highly qualitative and supplied in the right doses in order to guarantee the balance of the environment.

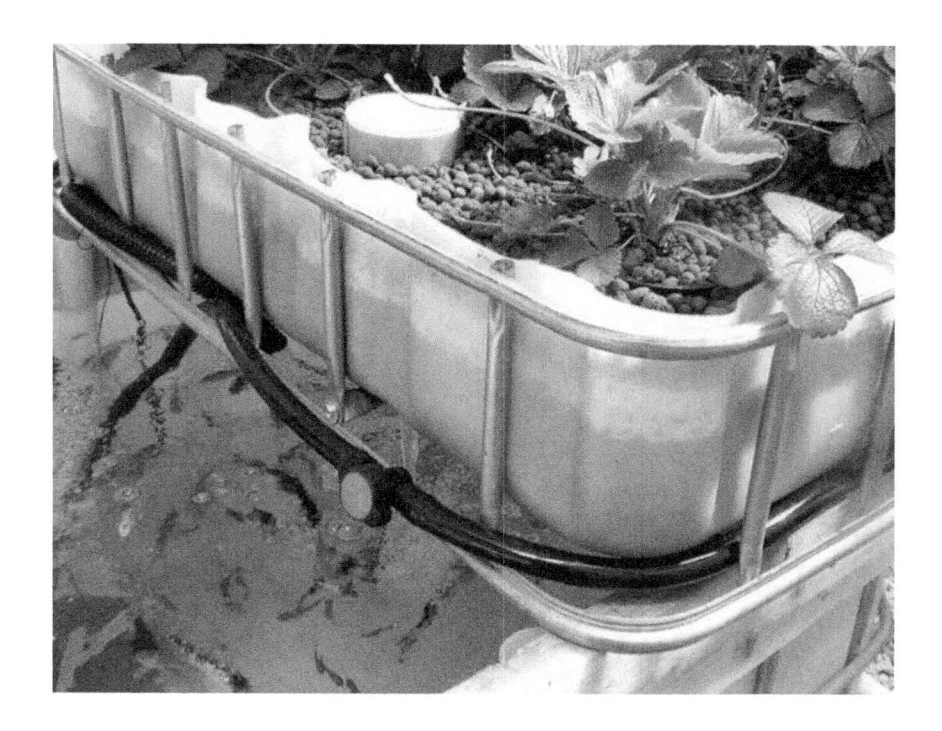

Chapter 8

HYDROPONICS VS AEROPONICS

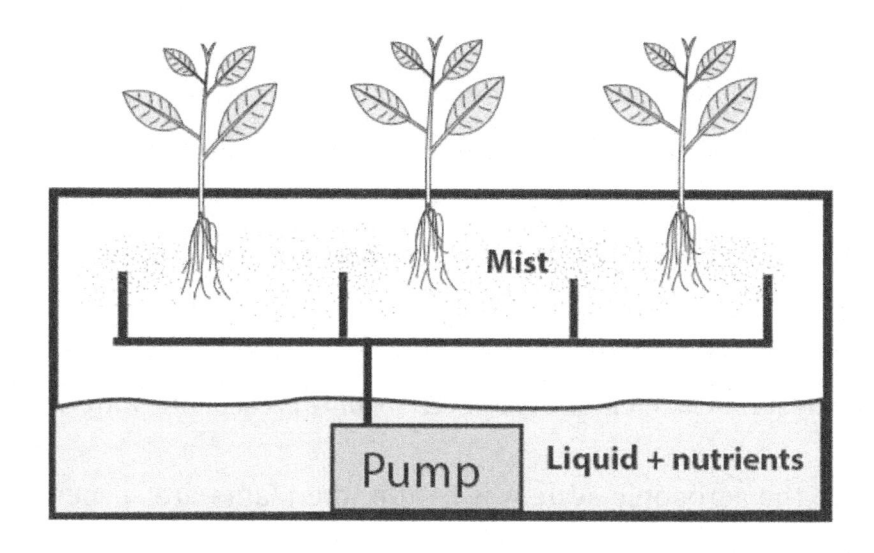

In hydroponic cultivation, as mentioned several times, plants are grown in the absence of land and with the use of water. In general, it is possible to say that with this technique, plants grow thanks to the action of water enriched with nutrients. In a first period, the plants are started inside inert substrates, such as coconut fiber, perlite, expanded clay, or other materials useful for the realization of substrates, to then pass into hydroponic systems, which provide, in addition to correct water supply, thanks to the presence of ad hoc lamps, the temperature, humidity and the right ventilation of the environment.

Aeroponics is an alternative form of growing plants, vegetables, and fruits that do not require the use of land or water.

With this cultivation technique, plants live and grow brilliantly and healthy thanks to the nebulization of a nutrient solution, based on water and substances useful for growth, which is delivered to the roots with a special spray.

This technique should not be confused with hydroponics, where the most crucial element is not air, as in this case, but water.

Once the aeroponic system is set up, the plants are suspended with the roots in the air inside a grow room (or cultivation chamber) where they will remain until the moment of collection.

The basis of growth and plant health is undoubtedly the constant control of temperature, humidity, and lighting.

Pros and Cons of Hydroponics

We have already said several times that the advantages of using a hydroponic system certainly concern reduced maintenance, the possibility of cultivating at any time of the year, and the opportunity to control the climate of the cultivation environment.

More generally, the great advantage of hydroponics is in complete control over nutrients and, therefore, on the growth of plants. Furthermore, hydroponically grown plants perform better than plants grown in the soil. Many systems of this type recycle water and reduce waste.

These soil-free cultivation systems use only 10% of the amount of water needed for conventional crops and are fairly easy to build and assemble. Hydroponic gardens do not require the use of herbicides or pesticides, precisely because weeds do not grow there, they need little space and do not depend on the growing seasons, because they use lamplight, which can be installed anywhere.

However, hydroponic gardens have some cons; for example, if the temperature is too high or too low, even for a single day, the plants could die or otherwise suffer severe damage. Also, the purchase of hydroponic systems and accessories may require a significant expense, especially if you are not an expert.

Pros and Cons of Aeroponics

Among the advantages of aeroponics, there is, in the absolute first place, the efficiency and cleanliness of the cultivation environment.

With this technique, excellent and thriving crops are obtained in a short period. Another significant advantage is the slight risk of contracting bacterial diseases and infections. On the other hand, a disadvantage, especially if you are a beginner, lies in the rather high cost, because it requires the purchase of a series of equipment. Also, it is necessary to have a dedicated indoor room, where you can install the aeroponic system.

Hydroponics and Aeroponics: similarities and differences

The hydroponic and aeroponic systems have many points in common: aeroponics is, in reality, a particular type of hydroponic culture, which also uses the benefits of air. To simplify and summarize, we can say that aeroponics is an evolution of hydroponics, to get the most out of the potential of plants in terms of yield and speed.

The main difference between the two techniques is that hydroponic systems come in many forms: plants can be suspended in water full time, or a continuous or intermittent flow can feed them. In a hydroponic system, plants grow with water and without soil, with the help of inert substrates. The two systems have in common the supply of nutrients that are delivered directly from the source and supplied to the roots.

The plants in aeroponics, however, are never placed in the water but sprayed at a distance thanks to a dispenser that hydrates and nourishes the roots several times an hour, thanks to an automated system that guarantees regularity and punctuality. One reason these two cultivation methods have so much in common is that aeroponics is, in reality, a type of hydroponics. The main difference is that hydroponic systems can be of various types: there are different types, and for this, you can choose the one that best suits your needs.

A disadvantage common to both hydroponic and aeroponic cultivation systems is that relying on automated systems that require, therefore, electricity, they could require the use of expensive generators to be used in case of power outages. However, once set up and started, hydroponic and aeroponic systems allow you to save significantly compared to traditional cultivation techniques.

According to current phenomena, it is possible that forms of hydroponic and aeroponic agriculture will increase in popularity over time and become commonplace in all of our homes. What is certain is that due to climate change and the unregulated action of man, the quantity of soil available for cultivation will tend to decrease, and its quality will continue to deteriorate. Therefore more and more people will try to produce healthy food in their homes (many have already started to grow salads, tomatoes, strawberries, etc.). Hydroponic and aeroponic gardens and orchards can provide the right answer to these growing needs.

Chapter 9

IT'S TIME TO TRY!

Building a hydroponic system is a great adventure.

At first, everything may seem complicated, and there is a lot of information to assimilate, but now you have the basis for doing it.

Research, study, design, and modify according to your needs.

With the hydroponic system, cultures grow very fast, allowing you to test, experiment, do, and modify quickly.

And once you find yourself in a thousand shades of green, you will surely be rewarded for every effort made.

Good Luck And Good Growth!

Made in the USA
Middletown, DE
10 April 2020